AGAINST ALL GODS

OBERON MASTERS SERIES

A C Grayling

AGAINST ALL GODS

*Six Polemics on Religion
and an Essay on Kindness*

OBERON BOOKS
LONDON

First published in 2007 by Oberon Books Ltd
521 Caledonian Road, London N7 9RH
Tel: 020 7607 3637 / Fax: 020 7607 3629
e-mail: info@oberonbooks.com
www.oberonbooks.com

Reprinted 2007, 2008, 2010

A catalogue record for this book is available from the
British Library.

ISBN: 1 84002 728 2 / 978-1-84002-728-0

Printed in Great Britain by CPI Antony Rowe, Chippenham

Contents

I

Introduction

DOES RELIGION DESERVE RESPECT? I argue that it deserves no more respect than any other viewpoint, and not as much as most.

Is religion really resurgent, or is this an illusion masking the real truth, that we are witnessing its death throes? I argue that, all appearances to the contrary, we might well be witnessing its demise.

What are the real meanings of 'atheist,' 'secularist' and 'humanist'? The words denote importantly different concepts, but get bandied about as if they were synonyms. I seek to explain them properly here.

Religious apologists charge the non-religious with being 'fundamentalist' if they attack religion too robustly, without seeming to notice the irony of employing, as a term of abuse, a word which principally applies to the too-common tendencies of their own outlook. Can a view which is not a belief but a rejection of a certain kind of belief really be 'fundamentalist'? Of course not; but there is more to be said too.

And: what is a humanist ethical outlook, apart from being one that does not start from belief in supernatural agencies? I sketch the outlines of this rich, warm and humane view in the concluding essay here, to offer the alternative to a religious outlook, an alternative that comes from the great tradition of Western philosophy.

Public debate about matters of moment takes place mainly in newspapers and magazines and on radio and television, and the nature of these media imposes limits on how long (not very long), how detailed (not very detailed) and how complicated (not very complicated) contributions to the debate can be. This often has the effect of over-simplifying and polarising matters too far, but it need not: it is not impossible to make one's case economically and clearly, though it is inevitable that those who cannot tell the difference between a concise and intelligible expression of a view, on the one hand, and on the other a merely simple and even simplistic view, like to call the former the latter if they disagree with it. Such is life.

The six polemical essays to follow, and the concluding essay outlining what a non-religious ethics looks like, all began life as journalistic contributions – with aspirations to concision and clarity – to the debate society is currently having with itself about religion. I subscribe to a non-religious outlook, and criticise religions both as belief systems and as institutional phenomena which, as the dismal record of history and the present both testify, have done and continue to do much harm to the world, whatever good can be claimed for them besides. The debate has become an acerbic one – and worse: some contributors to it have their say with bombs – but the following thought governs my own part in it: that all who have secure grounds for their views should not be afraid of robust challenge and criticism; if they are confident in their views they should be able to shrug off satire and mockery. The more insecure people are, the less confident they feel, the less mature their outlook is, the angrier they are made by what they label 'offence' to their religious sensitivities – even to the point of violence. They undermine and refute themselves thus.

Apologists for faith are an evasive community, who seek to avoid or deflect criticism by slipping behind the abstractions of higher theology, a mist-shrouded domain of long words, superfine distinctions and vague subtleties, in some of which God is nothing ('no-thing, not-a-thing') and does not even exist ('but

is still the condition of the possibility of existence'
– one could go on) – in short, sophistry, as it would
be called by those who have attempted a study of
real masterworks of philosophy, for example in the
writings of Aristotle and Kant. But those who would
escape into clouds of theology for their defence miss
the point made by religion's critics. The great mass of
religious folk believe in something far more basic and
traditional than the vaporous inventions of theology,
and it is on this that they repose their trust, and for
which some – too many – kill and die ('faith is what
I die for, dogma is what I kill for'). Moreover, the
deeply forested hideaways of theology start from the
same place as ordinary superstitious faith, so laying
an axe to this root brings it down too.

But religion is not theology; it is the practice and
outlook of ordinary people into most of whom supernaturalistic beliefs and superstitions were inculcated
as children when they could not assess the value of
what they were being sold as a world view; and it is
the falsity of this, and its consequences for a suffering
world, that critics attack.

This applies also to those who point to the comfort
and solace religions bring to the lonely, the old, the
fearful and the ill, even – they sometimes say – if it is
false. Well: leave aside the comfort and solace brought

to the suicide bomber who thinks he has earned all his family a free pass to heaven, and himself the post-humous ministrations of seventy-two ever-renew-ing virgins, and think only of the comfort religions provide 'even if false'. Would we tolerate the govern-ment telling us comforting lies about, say, an accident at a nuclear plant, or a spillage of deadly viruses from a laboratory? No? Then comforting lies have their limits. More importantly, is truth less important than comfort, even for the lonely and afraid? Are there not truthful ways to comfort them from the resources of human compassion? There certainly are. Given the crucial, inestimable, ultimate value of truth, would these not be far better than lies, however comforting? They certainly would.

And art – Raphael's Madonnas, Bach's sacred can-tatas, exquisitely decorated psalters and Qu'rans, York Minster and the Blue Mosque of Istanbul – where would art be without religion? It would be exactly where it is now. Art is the outpouring of the human heart; its skill is human skill, it is the effulgence of the creativity, delight, passion and yearning of the human mind. When our gods were dogs and cats, in Egypt, people made exquisite effigies of dogs and cats, and painted them in their elegance on tomb walls. When gods lived in the clouds on Olympus, people built wonderful temples with marvellously wrought reliefs around their pediments, depicting Athene and Hermes, Zeus and Apollo. Since the Renaissance when patrons other than the church were wealthy enough to commission nudes, landscapes, portraits, hunting scenes, records of battles and still lifes, people enlarged the scope of art and celebrated everything – everything human, everything about the world inhabited and enjoyed by humanity. People have never really done anything else: Handel's oratorios and the *Missa Solemnis* are music, made and sung by people for the joy of other people, as much if not more than they are decorations for superstition.

The polemics to follow are brief and blunt. For longer and more detailed expositions and arguments of the point of view they express, I invite readers to consult my *What Is Good?* (Weidenfeld 2002) and *The Choice of Hercules* (Weidenfeld 2007). These two books are intended to argue the case for a non-religious orientation to the world, and its associated ethics of humanism, while in five collections of essays beginning with *The Meaning of Things* (Weidenfeld 2001) I seek to demonstrate how, across the range of art, literature, thought, science, history and life, such an attitude manifests itself in particularities. These remarks are intended to pre-empt critics of the brevity of what follows: if they think the following cases too quickly made, let them go to those seven books for the slower journey thither.

And if the tone of the polemics here seems combative, it is because the contest between religious and non-religious outlooks is such an important one, a matter literally of life and death, and there can be no temporising. It is in the final essay that a more characteristic tone, more welcome to myself, prevails; just as one would wish a more temperate and considered tone – and by far a kinder one – would prevail in the world at large.

2

Are Religions Respectable?

IT IS TIME to reverse the prevailing notion that religious commitment is intrinsically deserving of respect, and that it should be handled with kid gloves and protected by custom and in some cases law against criticism and ridicule.

It is time to refuse to tiptoe around people who claim respect, consideration, special treatment, or any other kind of immunity, on the grounds that they have a religious faith, as if having faith were a privilege-endowing virtue, as if it were noble to believe in unsupported claims and ancient superstitions. It is neither. Faith is a commitment to belief contrary to evidence and reason, as between them Kierkegaard and the tale of Doubting Thomas are at pains to show; their example should lay to rest the endeavours of some (from the Pope to the Southern Baptists) who try to argue that faith is other than at least non-rational, given that for Kierkegaard its virtue precisely lies in its irrationality.

On the contrary: to believe something in the face of evidence and against reason – to believe something by faith – is ignoble, irresponsible and ignorant, and merits the opposite of respect.

It is time to demand of believers that they take their personal choices and preferences in these non-rational and too often dangerous matters into the private sphere, like their sexual proclivities. Everyone is free to believe what they want, providing they do not bother (or coerce, or kill) others; but no one is entitled to claim privileges merely on the grounds that they are votaries of one or another of the world's many religions.

And as this last point implies, it is time to demand and apply a right for the rest of us to non-interference by religious persons and organisations – a right to be free of proselytisation and the efforts of self-selected minority groups to impose their own choice of morality and practice on those who do not share their outlook.

Doubtless the votaries of religion will claim that they have the moral (the immoral) choices of the general population thrust upon them in the form of suggestive advertising, bad language and explicit sex on television, and the like; they need to be reminded that their television sets have an off button. There are numbers of religious TV channels available, one more emetic than the next, which I do not object to on the grounds of their existence; I just don't watch them.

These remarks will of course inflame people of religious faith, who take themselves to have an unquestionable right to respect for the faith they adhere to, and a right to advance, if not indeed impose (because they claim to know the truth, remember) their views on others. In the light of history and the present, matters should perhaps be to the contrary; but stating that religious commitment is not by itself a reason for respect is not to claim that it is a reason for disrespect either. Rather, as it is somewhere written, 'by their fruits ye shall know them'; it is this that far too often provides grounds for disrespect of religion and its votaries.

The point to make in opposition to the predictable response of religious believers is that human individuals merit respect first and foremost as human individuals. Shared humanity is the ultimate basis of all person-to-person and group-to-group relationships, and views which premise differences between human beings as the basis of moral consideration, most especially those that involve claims to possession by one group of greater truth, holiness, or the like, start in absolutely the wrong place.

We might enhance the respect others accord us if we are kind, considerate, peace-loving, courageous, truthful, loyal to friends, affectionate to our families, aspirants to knowledge, lovers of art and nature, seekers after the good of humankind, and the like; or we might forfeit that respect by being unkind, ungenerous, greedy, selfish, wilfully stupid or ignorant, small-minded, narrowly moralistic, superstitious, violent, and the like. Neither set of characteristics has any essential connection with the presence or absence of specific belief systems, given that there are nice and nasty Christians, nice and nasty Muslims, nice and nasty atheists.

That is why the respect one should have for one's fellow humans has to be founded on their humanity, irrespective of the things they have no choice over – ethnicity, age, sexuality, natural gifts, presence or absence of disability – and conditionally (i.e. not for intrinsic reasons) upon the things they choose – political affiliation, belief system, lifestyle – according to the case that can be made for the choice and the defence that can be offered of the actions that follow from it.

It is because age, ethnicity and disability are not matters of choice that people should be protected from discrimination premised upon them. By contrast, nothing that people choose in the way of politics, lifestyle or religion should be immune from criticism and (when, as so often it does, it merits it) ridicule.

Those who claim to be 'hurt' or 'offended' by the criticisms or ridicule of people who do not share their views, yet who seek to silence others by law or by threats of violence, are trebly in the wrong: they undermine the central and fundamental value of free speech, without which no other civil liberties are possible; they claim, on no justifiable ground, a right to special status and special treatment on the sole ground that they have chosen to believe a set of propositions; and they demand that people who do not accept their beliefs and practices should treat these latter in ways that implicitly accept their holder's evaluation of them.

A special case of the respect agenda run by religious believers concerns the public advertisement of their faith membership. When people enter the public domain wearing or sporting immediately obvious visual statements of their religious affiliation, one at least of their reasons for doing so is to be accorded the overriding identity of a votary of that religion, with the associated implied demand that they are therefore to be given some form of special treatment including respect.

But why should they be given automatic respect for that reason? That asserting a religious identity as one's primary front to the world is divisive at least and provocative at worst is fast becoming the view of many, although eccentricities of dress and belief were once of little account in our society, when personal religious commitment was more reserved to the private sphere – where it properly belongs – than its politicisation of late has made it. From this thought large morals can be drawn for our present discontents.

But one part of a solution to those discontents must surely be to tell those who clamour for a greater slice of public indulgence, public money and public respect, that their personal religious beliefs and practices matter little to the rest of us, though sometimes they are a cause of disdain or amusement; and that the rest of us are as entitled not to be annoyed by them as their holders are entitled to hold them. But no organised religion, as an institution, has a greater claim to the attention of others in society than does a trade union, political party, voluntary organisation, or any other special interest group – for 'special interest groups' are exactly what Churches and organised religious bodies are.

No one could dream of demanding that political parties be respected merely because they are political parties, or of protecting them from the pens of cartoonists; nor that their members should be. On the contrary. And so it should be for all interest groups and their members, without exception.

3

Can an Atheist be a Fundamentalist?

IT IS ALSO TIME to put to rest the mistakes and assumptions that lie behind a phrase used by some religious people when talking of those who are plain-spoken about their disbelief in any religious claims: the phrase 'fundamentalist atheist'. What would a non-fundamentalist atheist be? Would he be someone who believed only somewhat that there are no supernatural entities in the universe – perhaps that there is only part of a god (a divine foot, say, or buttock)? Or that gods exist only some of the time – say, Wednesdays and Saturdays? (That would not be so strange: for many unthinking quasi-theists, a god exists only on Sundays.) Or might it be that a non-fundamentalist atheist is one who does not mind that other people hold profoundly false and primitive beliefs about the universe, on the basis of which they have spent centuries mass-murdering other people who do not hold exactly the same false and primitive beliefs as themselves – and still do?

Christians among other things mean by 'fundamentalist atheists' those who would deny people the comforts of faith (the old and lonely especially) and the companionship of a benign invisible protector in the dark night of the soul – and who (allegedly) fail to see the staggering beauty in art prompted by the inspirations of belief. Yet in its concessive, modest, palliative modern form Christianity is a recent and highly modified version of what, for most of its history, has been an often violent and always oppressive ideology – think Crusades, torture, burnings at the stake, the enslavement of women to constantly repeated childbirth and undivorceable husbands, the warping of human sexuality, the use of fear (of hell's torments) as an instrument of control, and the horrific results of its calumny against Judaism. Nowadays, by contrast, Christianity specialises in soft-focus moodmusic; its threats of hell, its demand for poverty and chastity, its doctrine that only the few will be saved and the many damned, have been shed, replaced by strummed guitars and saccharine smiles. It has reinvented itself so often, and with such breath-taking hypocrisy, in the interests of retaining its hold on the gullible, that a medieval monk who woke today, like Woody Allen's *Sleeper*, would not be able to recognise the faith that bears the same name as his own.

For example: vast Nigerian congregations are told that believing will ensure a high income – indeed they are told by Reverend X that they will be luckier and richer if they join his congregation than if they join that of Reverend Y. What happened to the eye of the needle? Oh – but that tiny loophole was closed long ago. What then of 'my kingdom is not of this world'? What of the blessedness of poverty and humility? The Church of England officially abolished Hell by an Act of Synod in the 1920s, and St Paul's strictures on the place of women in church (which was that they are to sit at the back in silence, with heads covered) are so far ignored that there are now women vicars, and there will soon be women bishops.

One does not have to venture as far as Nigeria to see the hypocrisies of reinvention at work. Rome will do, where the latest eternal verity to be abandoned is the doctrine of limbo – the place for the souls of unbaptised babies – and where some cardinals are floating the idea that condoms are acceptable, within marital relationships only of course, in countries with high incidences of HIV infection. This latter, which to anyone but an observant Catholic is not merely a plain piece of common sense but a humanitarian imperative, is an amazing development in its context. Sensible Catholics have for generations been ignoring the views on contraception held by reactionary old men in the Vatican, but alas since it is the business of all religious doctrines to keep their votaries in a state of intellectual infancy (how else do they keep absurdities seeming credible?) insufficient numbers of Catholics have been able to be sensible. Look at Ireland until very recent times for an example of the misery Catholicism inflicts when it can.

'Intellectual infancy': the phrase reminds one that religions survive mainly because they brainwash the young. Three-quarters of Church of England schools are primary schools; all the faiths currently jostling for our tax money to run their 'faith-based' schools know that if they do not proselytise intellectually defenceless three- and four-year-olds, their grip will eventually loosen. Inculcating the various competing – competing, note – falsehoods of the major faiths into small children is a form of child abuse, and a scandal. Let us challenge religion to leave children alone until they are adults, whereupon they can be presented with the essentials of religion for mature consideration. For example: tell an averagely intelligent adult hitherto free of religious brainwashing that somewhere, invisibly, there is a being somewhat like us, with desires, interests, purposes, memories, and emotions of anger, love, vengefulness and jealousy, yet with the negation of such other of our failings as mortality, weakness, corporeality, visibility, limited knowledge and insight; and that this god magically impregnates a mortal woman, who then gives birth to a special being who performs various prodigious feats before departing for heaven. Take your pick of which version of this story to tell: let a King of Heaven impregnate – let's see – Danaë or Io or Leda or the Virgin Mary (etc. etc.) and let there be resulting heaven-destined progeny (Heracles, Castor and Pollux, Jesus, etc. etc.) – or any of the other forms of exactly such tales in Babylonian, Egyptian and other mythologies – then ask which of them he wishes to believe. One can guarantee that such a person would say: none of them.

So: in order not to be a 'fundamentalist' atheist, which of the absurdities connoted in the foregoing should an atheist temporise over? Should a 'moderate atheist' be one who does not mind how many hundreds of millions of people have been deeply harmed by religion throughout history? Should he or she be one who chuckles indulgently at the antipathy of Sunni for Shi'ite, Christian for Jew, Muslim for Hindu, and all of them for anyone who does not think the universe is controlled by invisible powers? Is an acceptable (to the faithful) atheist one who thinks it is reasonable for people to believe that the gods suspend the laws of nature occasionally in answer to personal prayers, or that to save someone's soul from further sin (especially the sin of heresy) it is in his own interests to be murdered?

As it happens, no atheist should call himself or herself one. The term already sells a pass to theists, because it invites debate on their ground. A more appropriate term is 'naturalist', denoting one who takes it that the universe is a natural realm, governed by nature's laws. This properly implies that there is nothing supernatural in the universe – no fairies or goblins, angels, demons, gods or goddesses. Such might as well call themselves 'a-fairyists' or 'a-goblin-ists' as 'atheists'; it would be every bit as meaningful or meaningless to do so. (Most people, though, forget that belief in fairies was widespread until the beginning of the twentieth century; the Church fought a long hard battle against this competitor superstition, and won, largely because – you guessed it – of the infant and primary church schools founded in the second half of the nineteenth century.)

By the same token, therefore, people with theistic beliefs should be called supernaturalists, and it can be left to them to attempt to refute the findings of physics, chemistry and the biological sciences in an effort to justify their alternative claim that the universe was created, and is run, by supernatural beings. Supernaturalists are fond of claiming that some irreligious people turn to prayer when in mortal danger, but naturalists can reply that supernaturalists typically repose great faith in science when they find themselves in (say) a hospital or an aeroplane – and with far greater frequency. But of course, as votaries of the view that everything is consistent with their beliefs – even apparent refutations of them – supernaturalists can claim that science itself is a gift of god, and thus justify doing so. But they should then remember Popper: 'a theory that explains everything explains nothing'.

In conclusion, it is worth pointing out an allied and characteristic bit of jesuitry employed by folk of faith. This is their attempt to describe naturalism (atheism) as itself a 'religion'. But by definition a religion is something centred upon belief in the existence of supernatural agencies or entities in the universe; and not merely in their existence, but in their interest in human beings on this planet; and not merely their interest, but their particularly detailed interest in what humans wear, what they eat, when they eat it, what they read or see, what they treat as clean and unclean, who they have sex with and how and when;

and so for a multitude of other things, like making women invisible beneath enveloping clothing, or strapping little boxes to their foreheads, or iterating formulae by rote five times a day, and so endlessly forth; with threats of punishment for getting any of it wrong.

But naturalism (atheism) by definition does not premise such belief. Any view of the world which does not premise the existence of something super-natural is a philosophy, or a theory, or at worst an ideology. If it is either of the two first, at its best it proportions what it accepts to the evidence for accepting it, knows what would refute it, and stands ready to revise itself in the light of new evidence. This is the essence of science. It comes as no surprise that no wars have been fought, pogroms carried out, or burnings conducted at the stake, over rival theories in biology or astrophysics.

And one can grant that the word 'fundamental' does after all apply to this: in the phrase 'fundamentally sensible'.

4

A Rectification of Names: Secularist, Humanist, Atheist

IN THE FOREWORD to a document produced by the religious 'think tank' Theos, the Archbishops of Canterbury and Westminster, in a joint statement whose very existence does the latter great credit given that he officially thinks the former is a lost soul (traditional Roman Catholic doctrine says that there is no salvation outside the Church), iterate the claim that 'atheism is itself a faith position' – a weary old canard to be set alongside the efforts of the faithful to characterise those who robustly express their attitude towards religious belief as 'fundamentalist atheists'. This is classified in logic as an 'informal fallacy' known as a '*tu quoque*' argument. We understand that the faithful live in an inspissated gloaming of incense and obfuscation, through the swirls of which it is hard to see anything clearly, so a simple lesson in semantics might help to clear the air for them on the meanings of 'secular', 'humanist' and 'atheist'. Once they have succeeded in understanding these terms they will grasp that none of them imply 'faith' in anything, and that it is not possible to be a 'fundamentalist' with respect to any of them. I apologise to those who know all this of old, but evidently if our Archbishops remain in the dark about such matters, there must still be a need for patient repetition of – what else? – these fundamentals.

Secularism is the view that Church and State (religion and national government) should be kept separate. The first secularists were medieval churchmen who did not wish the temporal power to interfere in church affairs. Temporal government of religious affairs produces emasculated and feeble latitudinarian religious bodies like the Church of England (so this, if any religious body has to exist, is a good thing), whereas religious interference or, worse, control of government has a ready tendency to degenerate into what we might revealingly call Talibanism, as history and current affairs overwhelmingly and tragically attest.

If religious organisations had any sense they would embrace secularism as their best chance of survival, because a secular dispensation keeps the public domain neutral with respect to all interest groups within it, including the different religions and their internally competing denominations, allowing them all to survive – which they would not do if one became dominant and had the ear, or the levers, of temporal government.

As this shows, it is possible (and even wise) for religious people to be secularists too.

Humanism in the modern sense of the term is the view that whatever your ethical system, it derives from your best understanding of human nature and the human condition in the real world. This means that it does not, in its thinking about the good and about our responsibilities to ourselves and one another, premise putative data from astrology, fairy tales, supernaturalistic beliefs, animism, polytheism, or any other inheritances from the ages of humankind's remote and more ignorant past.

It is possible for religious people to be humanists too: though not without inconsistency or at least oddity, for there is no role to be played in a humanistic ethics by their (definingly religious) belief in the existence of supernatural agencies. Perhaps they need to believe in such agencies because they cannot otherwise understand how there can be a natural world – as if invoking 'Chaos and old night' (in one Middle Eastern mythology the progenitors of all things) explained anything, let alone the universe's existence. Doing so might satisfy a pathological metaphysical need for what Paul Davies calls 'the self-levitating super-turtle', but it is obviously enough not worth discussing.

'Atheism' is a word used by religious people to refer to those who do not share their belief in the existence of supernatural entities or agencies. Presumably (as I can never tire of pointing out) believers in fairies would call those who do not share their views 'a-fair-yists', hence trying to keep the debate on fairy turf, as if it had some sensible content; as if there were something whose existence could be a subject of discussion worth the time. People who do not believe in supernatural entities do not have a 'faith' in 'the non-existence of X' (where X is 'fairies' or 'goblins' or 'gods'); what they have is a reliance on reason and observation, and a concomitant preparedness to accept the judgement of both on the principles and theories which premise their actions. The views they take about things are proportional to the evidence supporting them, and are always subject to change in the light of new or better evidence. 'Faith' – specifi-cally and precisely: the commitment to a belief in the absence of evidence supporting that belief, or even (to the greater merit of the believer) in the very teeth of evidence contrary to that belief – is a far different thing, which is why the phrase 'religious think tank' has a certain comic quality to it: for faith at its quickly reached limit is the negation of thought.

So despite the best efforts of religious folk to keep the discussion on their turf, those who do not share their outlook should repudiate the label 'atheist' unless those who wish to use it are prepared to say 'atheist and afairyist and agoblinist and aghostist' and so on at considerable length, to mark the rational rejection of belief in supernatural entities of any kind. As Richard Dawkins has pointed out, since Christians and Muslims do not believe in Thor and Wotan, or Zeus and Ares and Hermes, or Siva and Vishnu, or the Japanese Emperor, and so endlessly on, they too are 'atheists' about almost all the gods ever imagined. Without the commonplace and dispiriting facts of history which show how religious organisations are in truth political, military and economic ones that exist for the sake of their all-too-human beneficiaries, it would not be easy to see why e.g. Christians believe in the volcano god of the Jews (the pillar of smoke by day, the burning bush on the mountain top), and why they choose the Jesus story out of all the many in which a god (Zeus and Yahveh are hardly alone in this) makes a mortal woman pregnant, who gives birth to a son, who engages in heroic endeavours, often involving suffering (think of Hercules and his labours), and therefore goes to heaven. For this tale is a commonplace of the old Middle Eastern religions, and it is arbitrary to pick this one rather than that one to kill and die for.

And on that subject: the sufferings attributed to Jesus, involving torture and an unpleasant death, all (so the putative records say) within less than twenty-four hours, are horrible enough to contemplate, but every day of the week millions of women suffer more and for longer in childbirth. Longer and worse suffering is also experienced by torture victims in the gaols of tyrannical regimes – and in the gaols of some democratic ones too, alas. Why then does Christianity's founding figure have a special claim in this regard? Flagellation followed by crucifixion was the form of Roman punishment particularly reserved for terrorists and insurgents in their Empire, and many thousands died that way: after the Spartacist revolt one of the approach roads to Rome was lined on both sides for miles with crucified rebels. Should we 'worship' Spartacus? After all, he sought to liberate Rome's slaves, a high and noble cause, and put his life on the line to do it.

G. K. Chesterton, one of the Catholic faithful, sought to discomfort non-religious folk by saying 'there are only two kinds of people; those who accept dogmas and know it, and those who accept dogmas and don't know it'. He is wrong: there are three kinds of people; these two, and those who know a dogma when it barks, when it bites, and when it should be put down.

Even some on my own side of the argument here make the mistake of thinking that the dispute about supernaturalistic beliefs is whether they are true or false. Epistemology teaches us that the key point is about rationality. If a person gets wet every time he is in the rain without an umbrella, yet persists in hoping that the next time he is umbrella-less in the rain he will stay dry, then he is seriously irrational. To believe in the existence of (say) a benevolent and omnipotent deity in the face of childhood cancers and mass deaths in tsunamis and earthquakes, is exactly the same kind of serious irrationality. The best one could think is that if there is a deity (itself an overwhelmingly irrational proposition for a million other reasons), it is not benevolent. That's a chilling thought; and as it happens, a quick look around the world and history would encourage the reply 'the latter' if someone asked, 'if there is a deity, does the evidence suggest that it is benevolent or malevolent?' Some theologians – those master-wrigglers when skewered by logic – try to get out of the problem by saying that the deity is not omnipotent; this is what Keith Ward attempted when debating 'god and the tsunami' in *Prospect* magazine. A non-omnipotent deity, eh? Well: if the theologians keep going with their denials of the traditional attributes of deity, they will eventually get to where common sense has already got the rest of us: to the simple rational realisation that the notions of deities, fairies and goblins belong in the same bin. Let us hope, in the interest of limiting religion-inspired conflict round the world, that they hurry up on their journey hither.

And then perhaps we can have a proper discussion about the ethical principles of mutual concern, imaginative sympathy and courageous tolerance on which the chances for individual and social flourishing rest. We need to meet one another as human individuals, person to person, in a public domain hospitable to us all, independently of the Babel of divisive labels people impose on others or adopt for themselves. Look at children in nursery school: a real effort has to be made to teach them, later on, how to put up barriers between themselves and their classmates on the basis of gender, ethnicity and their parents' choice of superstition. That is how our tragedy as a species is kept going: in the systematic perversion of our first innocence by falsehood and factionalism.

5

The Corrosion of Reason

A N OPINIONPANEL RESEARCH survey conducted in July 2006 found that more than 30 per cent of UK university students believe in creationism or intelligent design. This raw detail is gasp-inducing enough in its own right, as indication of the effect of the fairy-tales that once served mankind as its primitive science and technology in its intellectual infancy, and continue to assert a grip on too many. But it is even more troubling as a symptom of a wider corrosion, the spread of a more virulent cancer of unreason, which is affecting not just the mental culture of our own country but the fate of the world itself. If that last phrase seems hyperbolic, read on.

Take the local concern first, and ask what is signified by the 30 per cent statistic at issue. From the day that the government of John Major allowed polytechnics to redescribe themselves as universities, and his and successive governments set a target of getting 50 per cent of school leavers into higher education, but without the huge investment of resources at all levels that would make this viable, it was inevitable that standards required for entrance to degree level courses would fall. And so it has dramatically proved. At the same time standards in public examinations at secondary school level have also fallen, by some measures a long way. The official line, of course, is that the latter at least is not true: but such is the way with official lines.

The combined result is that a significant proportion of university entrants today are noticeably different from their average forerunners of a generation ago: measurably less literate, less numerate, less broadly knowledgeable, and sometimes less reflective. At the same time education has been infected by post-modern relativism and the less desirable effects of 'political correctness', whose combined effect is to encourage teachers to accept, and even promote as valid alternatives, the various superstitions and antique belief systems constituting the multiplicity of different and generally competing religions represented in our multicultural society. This has gone so far that our taxes are now arrogated to supporting 'faith-based schooling', which means the ghetto-isation of intellectually defenceless children into a variety of competing superstitions, despite the stark evidence, all the way from Northern Ireland to the madrassahs of Pakistan, of what this does for the welfare of mankind.

The key to the weakening of intellectual rigour that all this represents is that enquiry is no longer premised on the requirement that belief must be proportional to carefully gathered and assessed evidence. The fact that 'faith' is enough to legitimate anything from superstition to mass murder is not one whit troubling to 'people of faith' themselves, most of whom disagree with the faith of most other 'people of faith' (thus: a Christian does not accept Islam, and vice versa; so a Christian's claim to be certain, by faith, that his is the only true religion is rejected, on grounds of faith, by the Muslim; and so on, to the point of mutual assassination); which shows that the non-rational mindset underlying religious belief, an essentially infantile attitude of acceptance of fairy-stories, has not been affected by the best that education can offer in the way of challenging and maturing minds to think for themselves.

Example: ask a Christian why the ancient story of a deity impregnating a mortal woman who then gives birth to a heroic figure whose deeds earn him a place in heaven, is false as applied to Zeus and his many paramours (the mothers of such as Hercules, the Heavenly Twins, etc.), but true as applied to God, Mary and Jesus. Indeed ask him what is the significance of the fact that this tale is older even than Greek mythology, and commonplace in Middle Eastern mythologies generally. Why are they myths, whereas what is related in the New Testament (a set of texts carefully chosen from a larger number of competing versions some centuries after the events they allege) is not? Do not expect a rational reply; an appeal to faith will be enough, because with faith anything goes.

'With faith anything goes': here is why the claim that the resurgence of non-rational superstitious belief is a danger to the world. Fundamentalism in all the major religions (and some are fundamentalist by nature) can be and too often is politically infant-ilising, and in its typical radicalised forms provides utter certainty of being in the right, immunises against tolerance and pluralism, justifies the most atrocious behaviour to the apostate and the infidel, is blind to the appeals of justice let alone mercy or reason, and is intrinsically fascistic and mono-lithic. One does not have to look very far to find shining examples of this pretty picture in today's world, whether in the Middle East or the Bible Belt of the United States. The rest of the world is caught between these two appalling instances of basically the same phenomenon, so it is perhaps no surprise, though no less regrettable, that the infection should spread from both directions.

More regrettable still, though, is the fact that the civilised quarters of the world are not taking seriously the connection between the world's current problems and failure to uphold intellectual rigour in education, and not demanding that religious belief be a private and personal matter for indulgence only in the home, accepting it in the public sphere only on an equal footing with other interest groups such as trades unions and voluntary organisations such as the Rotary Club. This is the most that a religion merits being treated as, as the following proves: if I and a few others claim to constitute a religious group based on belief in the divinity of garden gnomes, should I be entitled to public money for a school in which children can be brought up in this faith, together with a bishop's seat in Parliament perhaps? Why would this be laughed out of court when belief of essentially the same intellectual value, say, Christianity, is accorded all such amenities and more?

I remind those who seek to counter with the tired old canard that Stalinism and Nazism are proof that secular arrangements are worse than religious ones, that fundamentalist religion is the same in its operation and effects as Stalinism and Nazism for the reason that these latter are at base the same thing as religions, viz. monolithic ideologies. Religion is a man-made device, not least of oppression and control (the secret policeman who sees what you do even in the dark on your own), whose techniques and structures were adopted by Stalinism and Nazism, the monolithic salvation faiths of modernity, as the best teachers they could wish for. When any of these imprisoning ideologies are on the back foot and/or in the minority, they present sweet faces to those they wish to seduce: the kiss of friendship in the parish church, the summer camp for young communists in the 1930s. But give them the levers of power and they are the Taliban, the Inquisition, the Stasi.

Give them AK47s and Semtex, and some of the fanatics among them become airline bombers, mass murderers of ordinary men, women and children, and for the most contemptible of reasons.

How far are the 30 per cent of students who believe in creationism or its proxy, intelligent design, from airline bombers? A very long way, of course; the latter are a psychopathic minority only. But the point to register and take seriously is that there is nevertheless a connecting thread, which is belief in antique superstitions and the non-rational basis of the putative values they represent, values which can lead in the extreme to mass murder, as the chilling jingle reminds us: 'faith is what I die for, dogma is what I kill for'.

As part of the strategy for countering the pernicious effects that faith and dogma can produce, we need to return religious commitment to the private sphere, stop the folly of promoting superstitions and religious segregation in education, demand that standards of intellectual rigour be upheld at all educational levels, and find major ways of reversing the current trend of falling enrolment in science courses. The alternative is a return to the Dark Ages, the tips of whose shadows are coldly falling upon us even now.

6

Only Connect

E. M. FORSTER'S MOTTO was 'only connect'. Responding to this injunction by putting together three items of the same week's news – the week in which these words were written – is an instructive exercise.

The first is the description in the journal *Science* of the process by which evolution produces new molecular machinery in biological systems by incrementally adapting existing structures to new purposes.

The second is a report in the science journal *Nature* of several well-preserved 375 million year-old fossils of a species intermediate between water- and land-dwelling creatures.

The third is the announcement of a parchment found in the Egyptian desert containing part of a second-century AD Gnostic document, described as 'the Gospel of Judas', in which the legendary betrayer is exonerated and indeed placed in a theologically privileged position because (so the document says) he was asked by Jesus to deliver him to the authorities in completion of his mission.

Which of these three items of news is the odd one out? If you think this is a no-brainer, remember the respondent in the quiz show who said that the synonym for 'blessed' occurring before the words 'thy name' in the Lord's Prayer is 'Howard'. Perhaps this might count as news too, to all those wishing to know the name of God.

There is a biochemistry professor at Lehigh University in the United States called Michael J. Behe, darling of the Creationists, who says that biological structures are 'irreducibly complex' and their existence can therefore only be explained by invoking a divine designer. This absurd argument, which alleges a mystery (the existence of complex biological structures) and claims to solve it by introducing an arbitrary and even greater mystery (the existence of a deity), has exactly the logical force of saying that the shapes of clouds are designed by Fred. (Who or what is Fred? Pick a legend to explain.)

As Karl Popper pointed out, a theory which explains everything explains nothing – and all the religions, otherwise in fierce competition with one another over the Truth, explain everything. Unless a theory specifies what counter-evidence would refute it, it is worthless. Good science invites rigorous questioning and testing; almost all religions, at least at some time in their history, have killed those who have questioned them. No wars have been fought over theories in botany or meteorology; most wars and conflicts in the world's history owe themselves directly or indirectly to religion. By their fruits, we are told, we shall know them.

A simple test of the relative merits of science and religion is to compare lighting your house at night by prayer or electricity.

The molecular evolution research focuses on hormone receptors. Hormones and their receptors are protein molecules that fit one another like keys in locks. By comparing specific hormone receptors in lampreys and hagfish, primitive species of jawless fish, with more evolved versions in skate, Professor Joseph Thornton and his laboratory co-workers at the University of Oregon were able to reconstruct the genetic evolution of the molecules in question, tracing their evolution to a common ancestral gene 456 million years ago. They found a receptor molecule which predated the existence of the hormone (aldosterone) for which it now serves. This offers evidence of how changes in a system exploit existing structures for new purposes, and therefore how greater biological complexity arises incrementally from less complexity.

Professor Behe, believer in supernatural agencies (a class that includes fairies, demons, unicorns, cthonic gods, angels and ghosts) whose alleged existence is inexplicable and untestable, and credence in which rests on ancient writings embodying the superstitions of mankind's early ignorances, called Professor Thornton's work 'piddling'. That is not an expression, presumably, that he would use to describe the – earth-shattering? – discovery of the Gospel of Judas in Egypt's desert sands.

7

The Death Throes of Religion

ON THE BASIS of apparently incontrovertible evidence, commentators of various persuasions, among them Eric Kaufmann, writing in *Prospect* magazine, John Gray, writing in the *New Statesman*, and Damon Linker, author of *The Theocons: Secular America Under Siege* (Doubleday 2006), are convinced that we are witnessing an upsurge in religious observance and influence.

Kaufmann relies on the weak argument that demographic trends will turn Europe into a predominantly religious place, John Gray seems to hope that this will be so, and Damon Linker is convinced that a 'theocon' conspiracy has so successfully captured Washington that the US has become a *de facto* theocracy – as one might say: the home of faith-based politics, faith-based science (creationism), faith-based medicine ('pro-life'), faith-based foreign policy (conducting jihad for American/Baptist values) and faith-based attacks on civil liberties. Add this to the all-too-obvious fact of political Islam – Islamism – and the case seems made.

But I see the same evidence as yielding the opposite conclusion. What we are witnessing is not the resurgence of religion, but its death throes. Two considerations support this claim. One is that there are close and instructive historical precedents for what is happening now. The second comes from an analysis of the nature of contemporary religious politics.

If a given interest group turns up the volume, it is usually reacting to provocation. We view the Victorian era as a sanctimonious period of improving movements such as self-help, temperance and university missions to city slums. But prudishness and do-goodery existed precisely because their contraries – poverty, drunkenness, godlessness and indecency – were endemic: some streets of Victorian London swarmed with child prostitutes, and were too dangerous to walk at night. In the same way, today's 'religious upsurge' is a reaction to the prevalence of its opposite. In fact, it is a reaction to defeat, in a war that it cannot win even if it succeeds in a few battles on the way down.

Here is what is happening. Over the last half-century, sections of the Muslim world have become increasingly affronted by the globalisation of western and especially American culture and values, which appears arrogantly to disdain their traditions. Yet latterly, some of these same sections of Islam have been emboldened by the victory of warriors of the faith over a superpower (Afghanistan's Mujahedin over Soviet Russia); the combination encourages them to assert their opposition to the engulfing encroachment of western modernity, even by taking up arms.

When a climate of heightened tension such as this prompts activists in one religious group to become more assertive, to push their way forward in the public domain to demand more attention, more respect, more public funds (faith-based schools are one example), other religious groups, not wishing to be left behind, follow suit. In Britain, Muslim activism has been quickly mimicked by others – by Sikhs demonstrating about a play, Christian evangelicals demonstrating about an opera, and all of them leaping on the funding bandwagon for faith and interfaith initiatives. To placate them, politicians lend an ear; the media report it; immediately these minorities of interest have an amplifier for their presence. The effect is that suddenly it seems as if there are religious devotees everywhere, and the spurious magnification of their importance further promotes their confidence. As a result they make some gains, as the faith schools example shows.

Yet the fact is that less than 10 per cent of the British population attend church, mosque, synagogue or temple every week, and this figure is declining in all but immigrant communities. This is hardly the stuff of religious resurgence. Yes, over half the population claim vaguely to believe in Something, which includes feng shui and crystals, and they may be 'C of E' in the sense of 'Christmas and Easter', but they are functionally secularist and would be horrified if asked to live according to the letter of (say) Christian morality: giving all one's possessions to the poor, taking no thought for the morrow, and so impracticably forth. Not even Christian clerics follow these injunctions. This picture is repeated everywhere in the West except the US, and there too the religious base is eroding.

The historical precedent of the Counter-Reformation is instructive. For over a century after Luther nailed his theses to Wittenberg's church door, Europe was engulfed in ferocious religious strife, because the Church was losing its hitherto hegemonic grip and had no intention of doing so without a fight. Millions died, and Catholicism won some battles even as it lost the war. We are witnessing a repeat today, this time with Islamism resisting the encroachment of a way of life that threatens it, and as other religious groups join them in a (strictly temporary, given the exclusivity of faith) alliance for the cause of religion in general.

As before, the grinding of historical tectonic plates will be painful and protracted. But the outcome is not in doubt. As private observance, religion will of course survive among minorities; as a factor in public and international affairs it is having what might be its last – characteristically bloody – fling.

8

The Alternative: Humanism

THE CURRENT QUARREL between religious and non-religious outlooks is another chapter in a story whose previous main incidents are to be found in the mid-nineteenth century and the early seventeenth century, in connection respectively with Darwin's discoveries in biology and the rise of natural science. Both are moments in the slow but bloody retreat of religion; so too is what is happening now. For, despite all appearances, we are witnessing not the renaissance but the decline of religion.

Here I wish to comment on something that, in the current climate of debate, has been mainly overlooked: the fact that those who are not religious have available to them a rich ethical outlook, all the richer indeed for being the result of reflection as opposed to convention, whose roots lie in classical antiquity when the great tradition of ethical thought in Western philosophy began.

For convenience I use the term 'humanists' to denote those whose ethical outlook is non-religiously based – which is, in other words, premised on humanity's best efforts to understand its own nature and circumstances.

Consider what humanists aspire to be as ethical agents. They wish always to respect their fellow human beings, to like them, to honour their strivings and to sympathise with their feelings. They wish to begin every encounter, every relationship, with this attitude, for they keep in mind Emerson's remark that we must give others what we give a painting; namely, the advantage of a good light. Most of their fellow human beings merit this, and respond likewise. Some forfeit it by what they wilfully do. But in all cases the humanists' approach rests on the idea that what shapes people is the complex of facts about the interaction between human nature's biological underpinnings and each individual's social and historical circumstances.

Understanding these things – through the arts and literature, through history and philosophy, through the magnificent endeavour of science, through attentive personal experience and reflection, through close relationships, through the conversation of mankind which all this adds up to – is the great essential for humanists in their quest to live good and achieving lives, to do good to others in the process, and to join with their fellows in building just and decent societies where all can have an opportunity to flourish – and where kindness and mutuality is the prevailing note of ethical interaction.

And this is for the sake of this life, in this world, where we suffer and find joy, where we can help one another, and where we need one another's help: the help of the living human hand and heart. A great deal of that help has to be targeted at the other side of what the human heart is – the unkind, angry, hostile, selfish, cruel side; the superstitious, tendentious, intellectually captive, ignorant side – to defeat or mitigate it, to ameliorate the consequences of its promptings, to teach it to be different; and never with lies and bribes.

Humanists distinguish between individuals and the wide variety of belief systems they variously adhere to. Some belief systems (those involving astrology, feng shui, crystal healing, animism…the list is long) they combat robustly because the premises of them are falsehoods – many, indeed, are inanities – and, even more, because too often belief in some of those falsehoods serves as a prompt to murder. Humanists contest them as they would contest any falsehood. But with the exception of the individuals who promote these systems when they should know better, humanism is not against the majority who subscribe to them, for it recognises that they were brought up in them as children, or turn to them out of need, or adhere to them hopefully (sometimes, and perhaps too often, unthinkingly).

These are fellow human beings, and humanists profoundly wish them well; which means too that they wish them to be free, to think for themselves, to see the world through clear eyes. If only, says the humanist, they would have a better knowledge of history! If only they understood what their own leaders think of the simple version of the faiths they adhere to, substituting such sophistry in its place! For whereas the ordinary believer has a somewhat misty notion of a father-cum-policeman-cum-Father Christmas-cum-magician personal deity, their theologians deploy such a polysyllabic, labyrinthine, intricate, sophisticated, complexified approach, that some go so far as to claim (as one current celebrity cleric does) that God does not have to exist to be believed in. The standard basis of religious belief – subjective certainty – is hard enough to contest, being non-rational at source, but this is beyond orbit. It is hard to know which are worse: the theologians who are serious about what they say in these respects, and those who know it for a game.

In contrast to the utter certainties of faith, a humanist has a humbler conception of the nature and current extent of knowledge. All the enquiries that human intelligence conducts into enlarging knowledge make progress always at the expense of generating new questions. Having the intellectual courage to live with this open-endedness and uncertainty, trusting to reason and experiment to gain us increments of understanding, having the absolute integrity to base one's theories on rigorous and testable foundations, and being committed to changing one's mind when shown to be wrong, are the marks of honest minds. In the past humanity was eager to clutch at legends, superstitions and leaps of credulity, to attain quick and simple closure on all that they did not know or understand, to make it seem to themselves that they did know and understand. Humanism recognises this historical fact about the old myths, and sympathises with the needs that drive people in that direction. It points out to such that what feeds their hearts and minds – love, beauty, music, sunshine on the sea, the sound of rain on leaves, the company of friends, the satisfaction that comes from successful effort – is more than the imaginary can ever give them, and that they should learn to re-describe these things – the real things of this world – as what gives life the poetry of its significance.

For that is what humanism is: it is, to repeat and insist, about the value of things human. Its desire to learn from the past, its exhortation to courage in the present, and its espousal of hope for the future, are about real things, real people, real human need and possibility, and the fate of the fragile world we share. It is about human life; it requires no belief in an afterlife. It is about this world; it requires no belief in another world. It requires no commands from divinities, no promises of reward or threats of punishment, no myths and rituals, either to make sense of things or to serve as a prompt to the ethical life. It requires only open eyes, sympathy and the kindness it prompts, and reason.